THE **PACIFIC CENTER**
FOR **WESTERN STUDIES**

at the UNIVERSITY OF THE PACIFIC
Stockton, California 95211

From
the Library of
Dr. and Mrs. Josef J. Shebl

Water Stone Sky

My heart is awed within me when I think
Of the great miracle that still goes on,
In silence, round me — the perpetual work
Of thy creation, finished, yet renewed Forever.

Bryant, "A Forest Hymn"

Water Stone Sky

A Pictorial Essay on Lake Powell

Stanley L. Welsh and
Catherine Ann Toft

Brigham Young University Press
Provo, Utah

Library of Congress Catalog Card Number: 73-20115
International Standard Book Number: 0-8425-0898-8
© 1974 Brigham Young University Press. All rights reserved
Brigham Young University Press, Provo, Utah 84602
Printed in the United States of America
74   5M   0003

Library of Congress Cataloging in Publication Data

Welsh, Stanley L
Water, stone, sky.

1. Powell, Lake.   I. Toft, Catherine Ann,
1950-   joint author. II. Title.
GB1625.U8W44   551.4'82'097925   73-20115
ISBN 0-8425-0898-8

To
All who look . . .
and see.

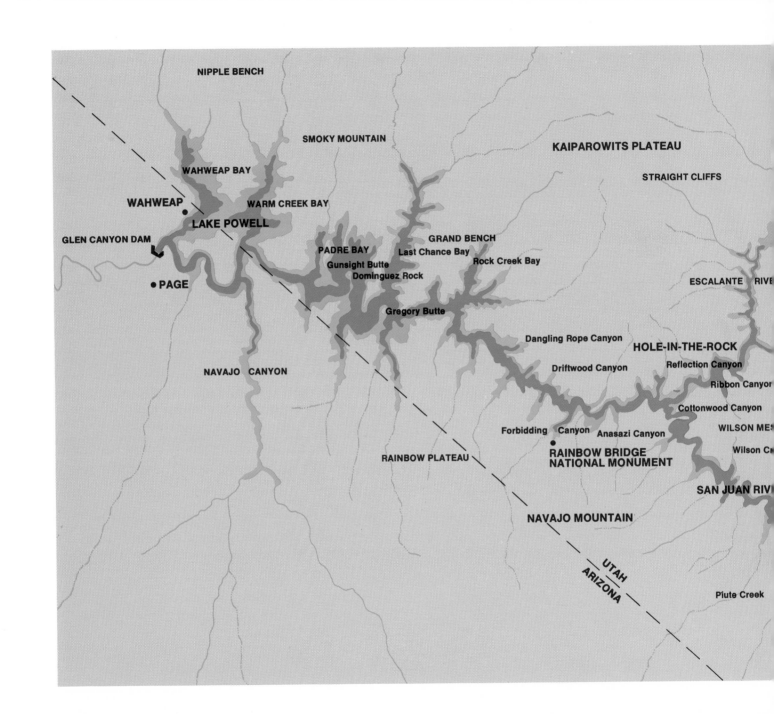

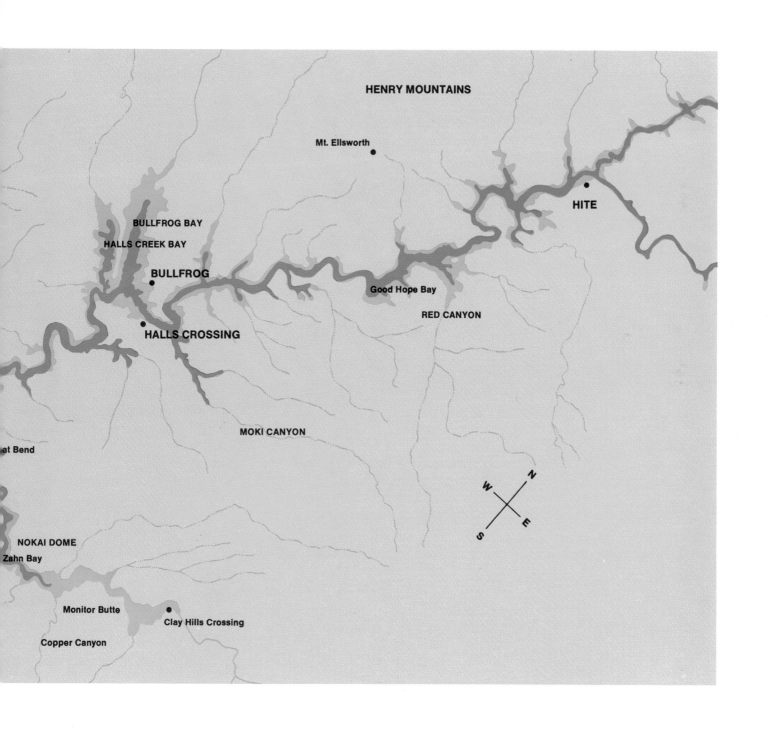

Contents

Preface

There are those who mourn the passing of Glen Canyon of the Colorado River — "the place no one knew." Burying the glens and alcoves, the grottos and narrow defiles — all temples of nature — the blue-black waters of Lake Powell rise more than 400 feet in the narrow inner gorge. Some of us never saw "the place no one knew," but we, too, can regret its passing. Even as we float on the lake's serene waters and watch the interplay of light on its reflective surface mirroring the pink sandstone, we think of the drowned canyon and its ghosts of desert gardens, hidden for an eternity by the massive depths. Even more, we think of the leashed river, the tempestuous Colorado, which embodied the violence of this harsh land, now a prisoner in the canyon of its own carving, its swift waters dissipated in the calm depths of the lake.

Lake Powell, like the land along it, is a paradox. At the same time that its waters have buried a canyon-land, stream bottoms, and other wonders, it has displayed a new world previously inaccessible to mankind. Skimming over its waters, we can discover an entirely different world than could such early explorers as John Wesley Powell. Some hundreds of feet above the canyon bottom, we can glide along cliff faces where

Powell would never have imagined a man could ever reach. Alcoves, shelves, and rocky ledges are now accessible, forbidden before to the human race by their impossible positions along a canyon wall.

Stepping over a cliff, a move which a decade ago would have meant death, now immerses us in the placid waters of an emerald pool. A swimming human form rippling the surface of the lake occupies a position previously restricted to flying things.

Mostly the lake fills only the narrow inner gorge. Above its waters rises a land of superb sandstone cliffs, a desert country both harsh and beautiful. Perhaps

Far left: Midday in winter at Reflection Canyon.

Left: Clear Day in autumn at Ribbon Canyon.

Right: Alcove at Hidden Passage Canyon.

there is not as much of this country as there once was — some elements are missing — but the remaining land beyond the water's edge stands in its superb, ethereal, natural glory. Reflected in the lake and stretching from it in the hazy distance is the slickrock country, undaunted by the brief instant since the lake was born — still "a place no one knows."

We dedicate this book to the beauty of Lake Powell, to an understanding of the features which bound its shores, and to a knowledge of the processes which produced this splendid region. Its intent is to record, in a small way, a portion of the

slickrock country along Glen Canyon as it now exists and as much of it existed in the ages before the land felt the presence of the modern world. Let us not mourn for Glen Canyon so much that our eyes are closed to the marvels of this rugged canyon country, marvels reflected in the exotic waters of an ephemeral lake. We should well mourn, however, if some future generation should accuse us of walking through this great land with eyes closed, allowing it to remain "the place no one knew."

Far left: Dominguez Rock at Padre Bay. Situated along the upper surface of a fin above a gigantic submerged meander is a lone rock. It is named in honor of Father Francisco Atanacio Dominguez who passed this way on November 7, 1776.

Left: Yellow sego lily (Calochortus aureus) at Wahweap Creek. The golden yellow petals of this sego lily stand in marked contrast to the gray detritis of the Dakota Formation.

Right: Monitor Butte near the east end of the San Juan arm.

Introduction

2

The region around Glen Canyon has traditionally been one of the most remote and most inaccessible in Utah and Arizona. Despite this fact, the canyon and its surroundings were penetrated very early by explorers preceding the period of the great westward migration. During 1776, the year of the founding of our nation, Fathers Silvestre Velez de Escalante and Francisco Atanacio Dominguez, Spanish priests, crossed Glen Canyon after they failed to reach California while traveling with a party "to discover a route from the Presidio at Santa Fe, New Mexico, to Monterey in northern California."

It was late in the season. Autumn had come, and trails were difficult to find. The party searched for a place where they could reach the river, deep in its protective canyon. According to historians, on October 26, 1776, the expedition reached the river, probably at the site of Lee's Ferry. Here they constructed rafts, but since the water was very deep and poles cut for the purpose of propelling the rafts would not reach bottom, the attempt to cross failed. Three days later Escalante recorded in his diary a statement which indicates something of the condition of the expedition: "Not knowing when we would be

able to leave this place, and having already eaten up the meat of the first horse, the pine kernals [*sic*], and the other provisions we had brought, we ordered another horse killed."

From their camp of October 29, Escalante, Dominguez, and party climbed to the escarpment which borders the lower end of Glen Canyon and attempted to find another approach to the river. Through Wahweap, Warm Creek, and Gunsight Butte canyons they searched in bewilderment and awe in this vast technicolor land for a downward route. They camped one night near the base of Romana Mesa;

Far left: Wahweap Bay. An evening in winter.

Left: Gunsight Bay and Gunsight Butte east of Romana Mesa. In this vicinity Spanish priests Silvestre Velez de Escalante and Francisco Atanacio Dominguez were forced to cut a trail into the stone with an ax for the space of a few yards before horses and men could descend into the deep gorge in the Navajo sandstone.

Right: Nipple bench at Wahweap. A summer storm on the Straight Cliffs Formation above the Tropic Shale.

5

here, it rained during the night, and in the morning it was very cold.

Near Gunsight Butte they found an Indian trail winding through a narrow defile and leading into a deep gorge carved into the massive Navajo Sandstone. In one place the way was sufficiently precipitous that the horses could not descend, even though the men were walking and leading them. Steps were cut into the stone with an ax for a few yards, and the party continued. Finally, on November 7, 1776, in a wild, remote, and desolate region, they found a place where the river ran very wide, where Indians had crossed

since time immemorial. This place was later designated as "El Vado de los Padres," or Crossing of the Fathers.

The river was very broad and ran not too swiftly at the ford so that the men and their animals were able to wade it without swimming. The journey beyond the river was almost as difficult as that in reaching it, but the expedition finally arrived at Santa Fe on New Year's Day of 1777.

Almost a century later, on August 3, 1869, John Wesley Powell's party, in boats deep within the canyon, reached the point where Escalante and Dominguez had crossed the Colorado River. Powell recorded a

Left: Cloudy sky of autumn near the Confluence. The layered clouds which precede an autumn storm change the mood to a somber one. The sandstone takes on a darkened cast as the sullen sky prepares to surrender life-giving water.

Right: Water over sandstone at Hidden Passage Canyon.

description of the crossing place in his journal:

A little stream comes down through a very narrow side canyon [Padre Canyon] from the west. It was down this that he [Escalante] came and our boats are lying at the point where the ford crosses. A well beaten Indian trail is seen here yet. Between the cliff and the river there is a little meadow. The ashes of many camp fires are seen, and the bones of numbers of cattle are bleaching on the grass.

Powell had entered Glen Canyon several days before, on the morning of July 29, 1869, after a difficult

journey through Cataract Canyon which is continuous with Glen Canyon to the north. The single sentence: "We enter a canyon today, with low, red walls," introduces the reader of Powell's diary to an account of Glen Canyon. Powell and his men were to leave the canyon at the present site of Lee's Ferry on the evening of August 4, 1869.

So it was that Powell spent almost one week in the canyon which he named after one of the features from within the rock-bound confines of the gorge: "On the walls, and back many miles into the country, a number of monument-shaped buttes are observed.

Far left: Water at Rainbow Bridge.

Left: Poison ivy *(Toxicodendron rydbergii)* at Escalante Canyon.

Right: South from Last Chance Bay. Autumn.

So we have here a curious ensemble of wonderful features — carved walls, royal arches, glens, alcove gulches, mounds, and monuments. From which of these shall we select a name? We decided to call it Glen Canyon."

Descriptions of the canyon by Powell are among the very best written about this vast region. The record of the canyon for August 3, 1869, is typical:

The features of the canyon are greatly diversified. Still vertical walls at times. These are usually found to stand above great curves. The river, sweeping around these bends, undermines the cliffs in places.

Sometimes the rocks are overhanging; in other curves curious narrow glens are found. Through these we climb, by a rough stairway, perhaps several hundred feet, to where a spring bursts out from under an overhanging cliff and where cottonwoods and willows stand, while along the curves of the brooklet oaks grow, and other rich vegetation is seen, in marked contrast to the general appearance of naked rock. We call these Oak Glens.

Apparent barrenness along the great canyon is deceiving, for the land supports an abundance of

Far left: Sunlight at Escalante Canyon.

Left: Cottonwood tree *(Populus fremontii)* in an oak glen near the Confluence.

Right: Falls in a small alcove during a spring storm — near the Confluence.

living things both plant and animal. The plants of the arid lands are widely and irregularly spaced, with much bare ground between. Also, because of their dark gray to gray-green color, the plants tend to blend with the background. The only really green places occur along the water courses and around seeps and springs. Here, there is an abundance of living things, supported by life-giving water, usually in short supply away from the edge of these perpetually wet places.

Powell and his men suffered from the monotony of their food, which deteriorated in quality and diminished in quantity each day. However, a brief

respite occurred on July 27, 1869, in Cataract Canyon:

Late in the afternoon we pass to the left around a sharp point . . ., and discover a flock of mountain sheep on the rocks more than a hundred feet above us. We land quickly out of sight, and away go all the hunters with their guns, for the sheep have not discovered us. Soon we hear firing. . . . One sheep has been killed, and two of the men are still pursuing them. In a few minutes we hear firing again, and the next moment down came the flock clattering over the rocks within 20 yards of us. One of the hunters seizes his gun and

Far left: Pink pricklypear cactus (*Opuntia polyacantha)* at Forbidding Canyon.

Left: Indian paintbrush *(Castilleja chromosa)* at the Confluence.

Right: Redbud *(Cercis occidentalis)* at Alcove Canyon, Great Bend of the San Juan.

brings a second sheep down, and the next minute the remainder of the flock is lost behind the rocks. . . . We lash our prizes to the deck of one of the boats and go on for a short distance; but fresh meat is too tempting for us, and we stop early to have a feast. And a feast it is. Two fine young sheep. We care not for bread or beans or dried apples tonight; coffee and mutton are all we ask.

Mountain sheep still are found along the plateaus and canyons bordering Glen Canyon, mainly eastward on Wilson Mesa. The sighting of a desert bighorn is reason for celebration because their numbers

have dwindled since Powell's time. Deer browse on vegetation in the side canyons, where beaver still gnaw the cottonwood trees and build small dams across the tiny streams. Skunk, gray fox, coyote, and badger are the most common carnivores; but on the plateaus and in canyons at higher elevations cougars still pursue deer and other game.

Indians had inhabited Glen Canyon for centuries before Powell floated through its dark reaches. Evidence of the earlier presence of Indians is found in such items as a bit of corrugated jar near a permanent pool in an alcove and arrowheads and chipped

Far left: Leopard frog *(Rana pipiens)* in Reflection Canyon. We find it pleasant to hear the occasional splat of a frog breaking the almost overwhelming silence.

Left: Porcupine *(Erithizon dorsatum)* at Reflection Canyon. One morning we followed quill-brushed footprints through the camp to a porcupine in an oak tree nearby.

Right: Artifacts at Cedar Mountain. A bit of corrugated jar, arrowheads, and chipped fragments of chert are evidences of the earlier presence of Indians.

fragments of chert along the mesas and shelves near the canyon. Small dwellings with T-shaped doors, tucked neatly into alcoves, mostly those which face toward the south, give testimony of a more permanent occupation. Civilization penetrated into the region with the advent of an agricultural Indian society dependent on corn, beans, and squash.

That civilization flourished for half a millennium and then retreated southward before Columbus discovered America. The land then served as a hunting ground for the wandering peoples who lived in a meager way in this difficult land.

early a decade after Powell had traversed Glen Canyon, in the autumn of 1879, another party gathered alongside this barrier. The expedition became known as the Hole-in-the-Rock party. They are referred to again later in this book, but they must be mentioned here also. To that group, Glen Canyon was simply a mighty barrier, an obstacle, to be crossed at a price. The crossing was a means to an end, "a short cut," a way to reach a goal which was eastward along the San Juan River. That the Hole-in-the-Rock party was successful is a tribute to the endurance, cooperation, and zeal of the people in the expedition.

Left: Hole-in-the-Rock. A morning in autumn. Wagonloads of Mormon men, women, and children with their livestock and gear lowered themselves into the depths of the inner gorge through this crack in a cliff face. Later they traveled along pastel-pink canyon rims, soft looking but as hard to pass over as life itself was for that hardy bunch.

Right: Hole-in-the-Rock in the spring of 1962. Platte D. Lyman, a leader of the Hole-in-the-Rock expedition, determined the grade of the road downward from the hole by using a square and a level.

17

And the story of their task is an example of people doing their very best under conditions of hardship and of sharing a common cause. Their backs were against a wall; it had snowed in the mountains behind them, closing the passes, and they had to arrive along the San Juan River before the spring planting season.

Powell and his men were similarly united by the hardship of their journey. In 1895, Powell wrote a preface to his *Canyons of the Colorado.* He recognized the men who had accompanied him and paid tribute to them:

Many years have passed since the exploration, and those who were boys with me are — ah, most of them are dead, and the living are gray with age. Their bronzed, hardy, brave faces come before me as they appeared in the vigor of life; their lithe but powerful forms seem to move around me; and the memory of the men and their heroic deeds, the men and their generous acts, overwhelms me with a joy that seems almost a grief, for it starts a fountain of tears. I was a maimed man; my right arm was gone; and these brave men, these good men, never forgot it. In every danger my safety was their first care, and in every waking hour

Far left: An oak glen at an unnamed canyon north of Ribbon Canyon.

Left: Spiderwort (Tradescantia occidentalis) at Forbidding Canyon.

Right: Moss on Navajo Sandstone in Ribbon Canyon.

some kind of service was rendered me, and they transfigured my misfortune into a boon. To you — J. C. Sumner, William H. Dunn, W. H. Powell, G. Y. Bradley, O. G. Howland, Seneca Howland, Frank Goodman, W. R. Hawkins, and Andrew Hall — my noble and generous companions, dead and alive, I dedicate this book.

Even before Powell launched his expedition at Green River, Wyoming, on May 24, 1869, the region on the west side of Glen Canyon had been visited by white men on several occasions. Stockmen were

Left: Cloudy day in autumn at Ribbon Canyon.

Right: Burros at Piute Canyon along the San Juan arm.

Far right: Morning in springtime at Ribbon Canyon.

grazing livestock — cattle, horses, and sheep — in the vicinity. Settlements had been established along the Escalante and the Dirty Devil rivers. But Powell made the region known in a scientific way by plotting the location of prominent features and by mapping the region.

Dreamers and schemers later attempted to utilize resources from the great canyon for personal gain, mostly failing because of low returns and high expenditures of time and energy.

Travelers utilized the canyon for a retreat, a place of solace, wherein their souls could be renewed,

21

where, because of privation, physical comfort did not have to come first, where timeless scenes were painted in unbelievable reds, browns, and blacks, and where forms of rock, softly rounded or sheer and smooth, glided past hour after hour in silent grandeur. It was, for them, a place of peace and restoration.

But civilization has caught up with this land which was previously considered to be almost worthless, and a great plug was placed within the inner gorge at a place where a beehive-shaped rock marks the west rim of Glen Canyon a few miles upstream from Powell's camp of the night of August 4, 1869.

Glen Canyon Dam is a monument to modern technology. Constructed at tremendous cost, the dam effectively stopped the flow of the river and turned the inner gorge of the canyon into a huge lake, named to honor the memory of John Wesley Powell.

The lake is an anomaly in an arid land. The loss of water by evaporation is tremendous, and an additional measure flows into the sandstone walls of its irregular basin. Silt from the Colorado and its tributaries falls out as the streams enter the quiet waters of the lake, and the basin has already begun to shrink by the volume of silt it contains. The life of any

Left: Rounded forms of Navajo Sandstone at Driftwood Canyon in midwinter.

Right: Glen Canyon Dam, with abutments in Navajo Sandstone. Glen Canyon Dam is a monument to modern technology. Constructed at tremendous cost, the dam effectively stopped the flow of the river and turned the inner gorge of the canyon into a huge lake, named to honor John Wesley Powell.

23

lake is short, depending as it does on the size of the basin and on the nature of the waters which enter it. The life of Lake Powell is limited to a few decades, perhaps a century or two, but assuredly the lake will fill with sediment. The gorge itself is mute testimony that a volume of rock equal to its size was excavated by the river, and now from upstream come the silts of ages, flowing in the relentless waters.

Left: Early morning in Driftwood Canyon.

Right: Warm Creek Bay at dawn. Late one evening, we launched the boat at Wahweap Bay and traveled south along the bay to the main channel of the Colorado River. We turned eastward and passed over the mirrored surface into the failing light of evening. At Warm Creek Bay darkness was complete except for the light from the star-studded sky. We moored the boat along a sandy beach and waited. Dawn turned the bay into a golden sheet.

25

The Canyon

Not all of the rugged and beautiful land lies beneath the surface of Lake Powell. The buried inner gorge, magnificent though it undoubtedly was, represents only a small portion of the canyon system of the Colorado River. Above the surface of the lake, along its shores, there is a land of superb technicolor geology, not masked by an imposing blanket of vegetation. On the whole, the shores are barren — often slickrock; more rarely a sandy beach occurs, but bare rock dominates. In few places of the world is the geology more spectacular. Here, red, pink, and white rocks abound, though elsewhere they are a rarity.

At first sight the landscape seems almost homo-geneous. The cliffs and talus slopes are bare and seem almost monotone, but a trip along Lake Powell affords the chance of a trip through time, along a cross-section of a portion of the history of the earth. Many layers of rock—sandstone, siltstone, and mudstone—are present, each unique in color, texture, composition, history, and age. Yet the sequence is an orderly one. The strata appear in the same order wherever they occur, and they change gradually from place to place. Cross-bedded sands give way to bedded ones, whites and buffs to reds.

Rock layers in the vicinity of Lake Powell, in the lower reaches of the Green and the former Grand rivers and along the massive Colorado River canyon formed at their confluence, are a series of alternating layers of differing thicknesses of mud or silt and sandstones laid down mainly in the Mesozoic era. Traces of Paleozoic rocks lie in the bottom of the gorge. Cenozoic rocks cap the highest plateaus of the great outer canyon system. The Green, Grand, San Juan, and Colorado rivers and all of their dendritic tributaries have cut a series of supercanyons, and in portions of two of these canyons lies Lake Powell.

Left: Haystack mounds of Navajo Sandstone along joint systems in a bend of the Colorado Canyon south of Cottonwood Canyon.

Right: Cliffs east of trail canyon at the San Juan arm of the lake. The massive Navajo Sandstone rests on the layered Kayenta, and this in turn rests on the massive, cliff-forming Wingate Sandstone.

31

High on alpine ridges of the Continental Divide, to the east and to the north, these rivers have humble beginnings as crystal clear brooklets trickling from melting snow fields. From the Green River lakes of the Wind River Mountains in Wyoming comes the Green River, from the north through the towns named Green River in both Wyoming and Utah. The Colorado, or Grand River, as it should be known, is born in Rocky Mountain National Park to the northeast, where the water from high peaks collects into Grand Lake. From there it flows as a modest mountain stream, growing until it meets the Green River deep within the canyon

south of Island-in-the-Sky in Canyonlands National Park. Here the two mighty rivers, the Green and the Grand, combine to form the greatest river of the region, the Colorado. Southward, along the northern side of the magnificent Navajo Mountain, the San Juan River joins the Colorado, coming from Wolf Creek Pass in the San Juan Mountains of southern Colorado, where its headwaters adjoin those of the Rio Grande, a great river which flows southeastward to the Gulf of Mexico.

A canyon such as that of the Colorado is much more than just the narrow inner gorge, which, with its dark reaches and troubled waters, forms perhaps the

Far left: Pothole arch in an alcove near the Confluence. Plunge basins form along the watercourses. They deepen with time, and occasionally one perforates through the thin edge of an overhanging ledge.

Left: Eastwood monkey-flower (*Mimulus eastwoodiae*) at Reflection Canyon.

Right: Navajo Mountain in winter. The summit of Navajo Mountain reaches skyward to 10,416 feet, about a mile and a quarter above the lake.

most intriguing portion. Eons of time have passed since the first water and silt from the juvenile Colorado River reached the sea. Its course finally became entrenched into the younger overlying formations. The tributaries cut laterally away from the main course, causing the retreat of those primeval canyon walls, and the first great series of cliffs were formed above the growing river. The retreat of phalanx upon phalanx of cliffs has been underway since that time. The canyon itself is evidence of its great antiquity.

Alternation of harder layers of sandstone with softer layers of mud and siltstone has allowed this

Left: Sandy basins in Navajo Sandstone near the Confluence. Depressions occur where the rock has been worn by water and wind. These support an abundance of living things. The sandstone surrounding the basins acts as a giant funnel concentrating the water from its large surface into the small depressions.

Right: Morning in late winter, west from north of the Confluence.

Far right: Wild four-o'clock (Mirabilis multiflora) on Cedar Mesa Sandstone, east side of canyon at Hite Bridge.

grand-scale canyon formation. The mud and siltstones are softer than the sandstones and erode more rapidly. The more rapid rate of erosion produces undercutting and causes the collapse of the resistant sandstone layers above, which fall away in massive slabs, often breaking away along joint systems within the cliff. Where joint systems are not present, the slabs break from the cliffs by means of conchoidal fracture, resulting in the formation of vast fan-shaped scars which take upon themselves the appearance of burnished metal after long periods of time. The slabs of sandstone break in falling, and for a time they

protect the angular slope of the softer underlying stratum. Regardless of the size of the slabs, however, they do not long remain. The angular boulders form only a thin mantle which is swept away a grain of sand at a time, as if the natural processes of weathering were loath to keep a house unclean — were loath to slow the process of the renewal of the earth. A boulder on a slope is destined to be unevenly deposited over a vast area of some future strata.

The fresh, bright faces of rock exposed as the slabs fall away change in time as they are affected by water, wind, sunlight, and changes in temperature.

Stripes of red water-washed sand and of blackish carbonaceous materials overlie desert varnish. These together merely ornament the patterned walls, and their basic design results from the nature of the cleavage of the rock.

R esulting from all these processes is a series of mosaic panoramas, from which one, limited only by the depth and breadth of his imagination, can create scenes. The size of the scenes in sandstone varies with the shape and size of the canyon walls. In places, unbroken tapestries are continuous along the great curves of stone above the meanders of the river and its

Left: Afternoon in autumn at Reflection Canyon.

Right: Wet sandstone in sunlight at the Confluence.

tributaries. In other sites, the mosaic ornamentation covers only a small area: a portion of an alcove or a gently curving wall. No two sections of a panorama are alike, and all scenes change in quality as light and shadows play about the summits and depths of the great canyon system. These tapestried walls require long periods of time for the ornamentation to reach some magnificent climax, and timeless as they appear, the length of their existence is not great.

Even the most splendid scenes fall, slab by slab, and the timeless painter again adorns the fresh canvas. The processes of nature are resolute in marking the landscape with scenes of magnificence.

Left: Register Rock. A mid-spring day along the pioneer road east from Hole-in-the-Rock.

Right: Morning. The entrance to Ribbon Canyon.

The Region

Lake Powell is situated near the south end of the Upper Colorado basin. The portion of the basin considered here is bounded on the north by the Tavaputs Plateau, where its southern escarpment comprises the Book, Brown, and Roan cliffs north of Price and Green River, Utah, and Grand Junction, Colorado. Surrounding the colorful middle portion of the basin are the massive Cretaceous cliffs of the Mesa Verde group of formations. On top of these are the Cenozoic formations, and these together make up the phalanx of cliffs, in places more than 100 miles wide, of the outer canyon of the Colorado. From between their bases erosion has removed uncounted thousands of cubic miles of material, grain by grain. The entire basin is a stage where the history of unending time has been played and will continue to be played.

Thrusting up through this series of sedimentary strata came fluid magmas, melting and lifting the formations, separating them and penetrating between them, not in one place, but in four. Resulting from the action of these volcanic intrusives are the islandlike ranges called LaSal, Henry, Abajo, and Navajo. On their flanks are canyons with streams carrying away both the solidified volcanic materials and the remnants

of the sedimentary formations which extend fingerlike up their slopes.

In some places other kinds of plastic bodies also moved upwards. Large accumulations of salt had been buried deep within the earth, trapped when ancient salt seas evaporated and were overlain by silt. Under tremendous pressure, masses of salt react as fluids. Flowing together they seek to rise upward, breaking through the seemingly impenetrable rock layers. Moving towards the surface, some of these salt accumulations finally were broached by the great river, and the salt was pirated downstream into the sea. The

Far left: Navajo Mountain in summer. Skunk, gray fox, coyote, and badgers are the most common carnivores, but on the plateaus and in the canyons at higher elevations, cougars still pursue deer and other game.

Left: Prince's Plume *(Stanleya pinnata)* on Organ Rock Formation at Hite.

Right: Mirrored image at Great Bend of the San Juan.

void left by the vanished salt did not persist. The unsupported formations settled as the salt was extracted, resulting in the formation of valleys such as Paradox, Spanish, Castle, and Salt, as well as Needles, Doll House, and Upheaval Dome.

Weathering does not occur at the same rate at all places. The region has received its name, Plateau Province, in recognition of its flat-topped monuments to time and to differential erosion. Mesas, buttes, spires — in fact all monoliths — are mere relicts of formations at the edges of the great canyon. Kaiparowits Plateau, Mesa Verde, Island-in-the-Sky,

Black Mesa, and Beckwith Plateau represent such remnants, and smaller features abound.

The age of the surface features is not necessarily the same because the retreat of cliffs exhibits the older underlying formations and because within the earth, forces are at play which have caused the strata to warp and to strain, to bulge and to fracture. Some regions have been warped upward and others downward. These changes affect the rate of erosion and display formations along some of the tributaries of the river — formations which can be seen elsewhere only within the deepest portions of the inner gorge.

Left: Spring day in Cottonwood Canyon.

Right: Waterfalls over Navajo Sandstone near the Confluence. The emotions aroused by the lake are difficult to pass off lightly: the poignancy after a rainstorm when curtains of water spill in lacy torrents over a cliff face, the exultation when waterfalls roar and thunder and splash into the lake.

Along the margins of the vast inner gorge, especially where the land alongside is of low relief, are terraces of water-washed gravels, sands, and clays. These were formed ages ago when the river was cutting at a higher level. The cobble is often flattened, with rounded edges, evidence that they have traveled far. Some of it had its origin in mountain ranges far to the east and north. Now the terraces are perched high above the level of the stream which deposited them.

Scenery, as we see it here, is the result of its history. Its beauty and grandeur reflect the timeless forces of nature in all their vast array. Man can only interpret and hope to understand that beauty.

Left: Yellow pricklypear (Opuntia polyacantha) at the Confluence. The pricklypears are armed, not only with long spines but also with very tiny hairlike spines called glochids. The glochids penetrate the skin easily, but they are so small they are hard to remove. They persist for a short time as a painful reminder of an encounter with this hardy plant.

Right: Padre Bay at sunrise.

The Stone

52

Northward from Lake Powell's southern end stands the escarpment of the Kaiparowits Plateau. Capping the plateau are the formations which comprise the Mesa Verde Group. The main strata of this group, visible along the higher portions of the plateau, are the Wahweap and Straight Cliffs formations, consisting of sandstones alternating with silts and muds which were formed as a series of barrier islands in warm seas of the Cretaceous. Quantities of coal are present within the Straight Cliffs Formation.

Beneath the strata of the Mesa Verde Group is the Tropic Shale which is transitional eastward with the extensive and very thick Mancos Shale. Both shales are very poorly cemented, and they weather quickly into gray clay. The surface of this clay is often marked by white encrustations of salts and is seldom obscured by the widely spaced plants.

Tropic Shale is a crumbly mass of magnificent colors dictated by the oxidation of its iron, mostly yellows and grays blending imperceptibly except where they are cut by some erosional channel; there in bold contrast, black stands out against yellow — soft, rounded, sensuous forms against a backdrop of cliffs and sky.

Bases of the Tropic Shale rest upon the thinnish Cretaceous Dakota Formation, also displaying thin layers of coal. The Dakota is seldom as much as fifty feet thick. From the lake the Dakota Formation is seldom visible. The Dakota is situated atop the coarse sandstone of the Morrison Formation or, where the Morrison is missing, directly atop the cliff-forming Entrada Sandstone. The Morrison Formation forms the stone caprock of the mesas and plateaus east from Warm Creek. The Entrada Sandstone is a thick and massive layer that is closely stratified in its upper members and cross-bedded in its lower portion. The

Far left: Tropic Shale. Benchland north of Gunsight Bay. The Tropic Shale is a crumbly mass of magnificent colors, dictated by the oxidation of its iron, mostly yellows and grays blending imperceptibly; softly rounded, sensuous forms against a backdrop of cliffs and sky.

Left: Cardinal flower (Lobelia cardinalis) at Reflection Canyon.

Right: Variegated butte at Padre Bay. The Entrada Sandstone changes from buff at Wahweap Bay to red at Dangling Rope.

cross-bedded part consists of ancient sand dunes now frozen in stone.

The Entrada Sandstone varies from chalky white with shades of rusty brown on its weathered surfaces north of Wahweap Bay to orange-red at Rock Creek. Between Wahweap and Rock Creek the chalky sandstone changes color, with tongues of white sandstone extending eastward for some distance along the formation. The smoothly rounded, hole-pocked, orange-red cliffs touching water's edge in Padre, Last Chance, and Rock Creek bays are Entrada Sandstone. The massive monoliths south and north of Padre Bay,

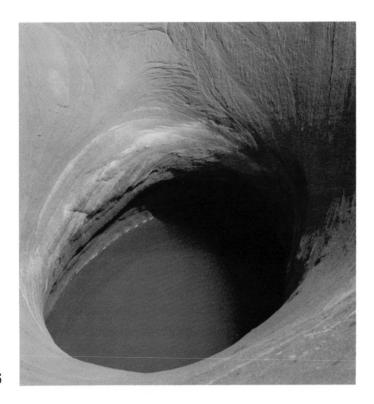

Left: Pothole in Entrada Sandstone at the north end of Padre Bay. Basins similar to this were important sources of drinking water for the people and animals of the Hole-in-the-Rock expedition.

Right: Jimson weed (Datura meteloides) at Reflection Canyon.

Far right: Head of Gunsight Bay from near Romana Mesa. The mesas and monoliths along Gunsight Bay are capped by the Morrison Formation. Below the caprock are the members of the Entrada Sandstone.

including Leche-e Rock, Tower Butte, Gunsight Butte, and Gregory Butte, are sculpted in the Entrada.

The Entrada lies atop a thin layer of gypsiferous, red mudstone which represents the Carmel Formation in this region. The Carmel is frequently obscured by talus, or detrital materials, which have fallen from the Entrada above it, but the Carmel is readily visible at many places along the lake.

East of Rock Creek the red Entrada, capped by the thinnish Morrison Formation, rises above lake level and forms a portion of the striking cyclorama north of Dangling Rope, Driftwood Canyon, and Forbidding

Canyon. Smaller, though by no means less beautiful, fragments of the Entrada are perched on the Carmel Formation along the outlying base of Navajo Mountain.

The base of Fifty-mile Mountain, the eastern escarpment of the Kaiparowits Plateau, is visible northward from Dangling Rope, from where may be seen all of the formations listed above, from the Straight Cliffs Formation down to the Navajo Sandstone.

The formations continue to elevate eastward from Forbidding Canyon. The vertical massive cliffs at waterside are Navajo Sandstone, cross-bedded and sculpted in rounded forms with canyons cut vertically

Left: Reflections in Driftwood Canyon.

Right: Rainbow Bridge. A summer day. A short distance from the mouth of Forbidding Canyon in a tributary which drains from the north slope of Navajo Mountain, a gigantic arch of stone bends gracefully over a narrow gorge from which flows a gentle trickle of clear water. The stone monument is a remnant of a slab of rock which stood in a meander curve of a stream and was cut through by the water.

and with alcoves and grottos marking the canyon sides. Desert varnish and streaks of carbonaceous materials paint the surface with scenes of charm and splendor emphasized by the conchoidal scars of slab rock long since worn to dust and distributed to the Gulf of California.

A short distance from the mouth of Forbidding Canyon, in a tributary which drains the north slope of Navajo Mountain, a gigantic arch of stone bends gracefully over a narrow gorge from which flows a gentle trickle of clear water. The stone monument is a remnant of a slab of rock in a meander bend of the

stream that flowed around the eastern edge of the slab. The waters cut away at both the upper and lower sides of the sandstone wall until a hole was produced, and the water flowed through this shortcut to the great river. This natural wonder was designated Rainbow Bridge. It is sculpted from the Navajo Sandstone which ornaments the northern base of Navajo Mountain like a clinging creature.

Near the confluence of the mighty San Juan with its graceful meanders, the Navajo Sandstone, too, rises above the lake level, and the bedded, maroon Kayenta Sandstone is revealed at the water's edge.

Left: Narrow-leaved yucca (Yucca angustissima) at Forbidding Canyon.

Right: Waterline on the Chinle Formation at Piute Canyon.

The Kayenta sits atop the most spectacular cliff-forming sandstone of them all, the Wingate. This formation shears off in tremendous rectangular blocks and forms almost vertical cliffs of great height. Only small portions of the Wingate are visible in the canyon of the Colorado between the confluence and the mouth of Escalante Canyon. The entire thickness of the Wingate is exposed in the vicinity of the Rincon. East along the San Juan River the Wingate rises above water level. Below it is the Chinle, a mass of varicolored muds and sandstones which are producers of uranium and which contain quantities of petrified

wood. Beneath the Chinle is the maroon-to-red, purple, white, or green stratified muds of the Moenkopi Formation. Below the Moenkopi, still older formations are exposed along the uplifts eastward along the San Juan and northward along the Colorado, and the same or equivalent formations are present along the canyon of the Colorado southward from Lake Powell.

Left: Conchoidal scar on sandstone in Escalante Canyon.

Right: Permian rocks at Hite Marina overlook. From the Rincon north to Hall's Crossing and Bullfrog Bay the rock layers dip gradually. North of Hall's Crossing the formations elevate. Near Hite the Navajo are rounded mounds atop the highest cliffs to the west, and at water's edge are the formations of the Cutler Group. The brick-red siltstones comprise the Organ Rock Formation, which rests upon the buff-colored Cedar Mesa Sandstone.

Reflections

The region is a difficult one for life. It is not passive (as some have suggested) but active in its relentlessness. One error of judgment might well be the last. Even those creatures which reside there, those to whom the region is home, are not immune to its dangers. One day during early September of 1971, a coyote lay on a talus slope between the shores of Lake Powell and the massive sandstone cliffs which stand wall-like back from the water's edge. The coyote was dead. We had witnessed its last few seconds of life. It had fallen from a narrow, gravelly ledge for more than a hundred feet in a gentle arc — almost as if in slow motion — while we gasped in horror and amazement and reached inwardly for some handhold. A wrong move on a ledge strewn with loose pebbles had cost the animal its life, and the day became a somber one for us. As we moved southward over the smooth surface of Lake Powell, we reflected upon the beauty of the scene, upon the harshness of this magnificent land, and upon the coincidence of the tragedy we had witnessed and the name of the canyon where it had happened — Last Chance.

Formidable are the cliffs, treacherous and forbidding to anyone traveling the area by land.

Nearing the confluence of the Escalante River from the south, we are reminded that if one is sufficiently daring and well prepared, even this once remote region can be penetrated successfully. There is a narrow defile in the Navajo Sandstone on the west side of the canyon known as Hole-in-the-Rock, a crack in the cliff face where, unbelievably, wagonloads of Mormon men, women, and children with their livestock and gear lowered themselves into the depths of the inner gorge. Incredible enough was that feat, but it was not enough. They ascended the other side, traveling along pastel-pink canyon rims, anomalous in their appearance—

Far left: Fish-hook cactus (*Sclerocactus whipplei*) on Chinle Formation, Zahn Bay.

Left: Canyon tree frog (*Hyla arenicolor*) at the Confluence.

Right: Natural bridge in Anasazi Canyon.

for as soft as they look, they are as hard to climb as life itself was to endure for that hardy bunch. Months later, in April of 1880, they drew lots for home sites at Bluff along the San Juan River, not because that was where they were supposed to settle but because they were too tired to go further. The almost impossible trek from Escalante to Bluff had required the entire fall of 1879 and winter of 1880.

The Hole-in-the-Rock party traversed the region when the aridity of the land was not overwhelming, but even then the constant search for water troubled them. Thinking of the sufferings of the people of the

Hole-in-the-Rock expedition, we can consider it almost a crime to glide along the saran-wrap surface of Lake Powell in shaded comfort, sipping ice-water. Alongside, the rounded red rocks arise from purple depths; behind, crystal waters part in a wake of jewel-drops tumbling from a ridge of foam, where the propeller churns the water. "Out there" it is hot, searing hot and dry; a short hike of a few hundred yards is enough to desiccate a man and make him dizzy from heat — to make him wish for the cold waters of the nearby lake. The opposite is true, of course, when winter chills the air and the lake is abandoned by all save the hardy few,

Far left: Collared lizard (Crotaphytus collaris) on Tropic Shale. The lizard was basking in the sun and posed for pictures as if it had been trained to do so. It was startled and left the scene, running at great speed on its hind legs, like a miniature Tyranosaurus.

Left: A waterfall at Wilson Creek, San Juan arm.

Right: Pink sego lily (Calochortus flexuosus) at Wahweap Creek.

those who seek after solitude and the beauty of clear air and who at that season cannot bear to take the plunge into icy water.

One should try both the hike beneath the sun and the plunge into frigid waters. It seems almost a necessity for understanding the real grandeur of the place — the essence of this canyonland of slickrock country. Is this comfort of a man-made lake, this ease of travel, of reaching a "stark and wonderful land" a desecration? Shouldn't our travel here have been as difficult as that of the Hole-in-the-Rock party, or at least as difficult as that of those in the Powell expedition of

1869 who floated here some hundreds of feet below where we now glide? Surely, the people of the Hole-in-the-Rock would have no such thoughts — not after months of grueling labor, of sweat and tears for each wearing step. One must suffer somewhat in order to enjoy what is good in life; pain allows you to know that you have lived.

I t is that kind of country — this slickrock land — the kind that puts conflicting thoughts in your head and disturbing emotions inside you. The land is no doubt a harsh one: heat and cold, drought and flood, wind and calm, starvation and plenty, life and death. No matter

Far left: Damselflies (*Odonata*) on driftwood near the Confluence.

Left: Water, stone, sky near entrance to Ribbon Canyon.

Right: White evening-primrose (*Oenothera caespitosa*) at Zahn Bay.

what happens, it happens in large doses. It is a land of pink, rounded forms appearing as soft as a baby's skin, of pastels of land and rocks and flower blossoms, of azure skies hung with rainbows after a violent storm of summer when eerie white clouds creep out of the gray and over the cliffs to skim down into the canyons. It is a huge, empty, lonely land, enduring, it would seem, everything, even the intrusion of Lake Powell, its massive waters burying for an eternity the innermost secrets of that deep canyonland. Indeed, it ignores us who dare broach the void of time and space. We are passengers on a doomed inland sea of exquisite beauty.

motions aroused by experiencing the lake are difficult to pass off lightly: the poignancy after a rainstorm when curtains of water spill in lacy torrents over a cliff face, the exultation when waterfalls roar and thunder and splash into the lake, the yearning when the early morning air is crystal amber and the sun pours lemon shades over the rocks and lake or when sandstone glows salmon under the waning moon, quarter full in the western sky. Perhaps (but it is hard to say) the fascination of the region reaches us most of all on a midnight when the landscape is ethereal and the full moon's light dapples the

Left: The straightaway southwest of Rock Creek Bay. At the end of the straightaway bordered by castellated cliffs stand the monoliths, the most distinctive of which is Tower Butte.

Right: Pour point with windblown waterfall near the Confluence. Rain trickled down the great sandstone surface and collected into streams which rushed headlong over ledges and cliff faces. The wind caught the falling water, turning it into a misty spray and carrying some of it upward, where it fell again on the sandstone.

surface of the lake and bathes the cliffs in silver shrouds, emphasizing the mysterious black of nighttime shadows.

The paradox involves a conflict between that which is, the present real world, and that which was or might have been. To experience it as it is brings sheer delight; to contemplate that which was is bittersweet. So it goes, this contemplation of charm and violence, of magnificence and disaster, of black waters and blue sky against a cyclorama of time — Lake Powell.

Left: Gregory Butte silhouette. Many landmarks occur along the lake. Each of them can be interpreted as animals, castles, cathedrals, or other objects.